COACHING WORKS

A HANDBOOK FOR CONTINUOUS SELF-DEVELOPMENT

Gus C. Baxter, ACC

Atlas Readings, LLC

Mahwah, New Jersey

How Life Coaching Works

Copyright © 2022 by Gus C. Baxter.

All rights reserved. No part of this publication may be reproduced, distributed or transmitted in any form or by any means, including photocopying, recording, or other electronic or mechanical methods, without the prior written permission of the publisher, except in the case of brief quotations embodied in critical reviews and certain other noncommercial uses permitted by copyright law. For permission requests, write to the publisher, addressed "Attention: Permissions Coordinator," at the address below.

Altas Readings, LLC

www.atlasreadings.com

Mahwah, New Jersey 07430

Ordering Information:

Quantity sales. Special discounts are available on quantity purchases by corporations, associations, and others. For details, contact the "Special Sales Department" at the address above.

How Life Coaching Works by Gus C. Baxter. —1st ed.
ISBN 978-1-0879-8613-5

CONTENTS

INTRODUCTION 7

WHAT IS LIFE COACHING? 12

THE EMOTIONS AS MESSAGES 24

SKILLS FOR GROWTH 35

THE 5 KEYS OF LISTENING 46

COACHING QUESTIONNAIRE 57

*Dedicated to all those who are passionate
about personal and professional development.*

Acknowledgements

This book has been a creative journey that reflects the last three years of growth, learning, and celebration. Coaching has been an incredible resource within my own life. I am honored to be able to work with so many incredible individuals through my own coaching practice. I am blown away by what my clients accomplish. I am truly thankful to my friends and family, who continue to support me through this amazing journey.

Thank you to Dr. Virginia A. Shea, Gus Baxter Sr., Margaret Baxter, Kathryn A. Freund, Douglas Slaybough, Courtney Donohue, Russell Donohue, Cassandra Gioffre, Kathryn Paturzo, Heidi Cooper, Joshua Voelpel, Dr. Ellen Reinhard, Alexandra Pollock, Garrett Goldfinger, Christina Pollock, Warren W. Veech, Dr. Carmen Renna, Lauren Hagan, Alessandra Conti, and Marcus Kain.

This book has been possible because of your support.

Introduction

"The beginning is the most important part of the work." – Plato

Life coaching is a powerful, action-oriented practice that creates incredible personal and professional transformation. Within my own coaching practice, I work with inspiring professionals from all walks of life. Their goals are as varied as their backgrounds. A new job, a new promotion, launching a small business, writing a book, discovering who they are post-pandemic, understanding what drives them and going all in – all of these are empowering, transformative topics for life coaching. Here is what some of these amazing clients have to say:

"One discovery discussion with Gus was incredibly helpful and we were able to outline my goals. You are in the driver's seat in terms of what you want to focus on and talk about, Gus is simply there to offer options on your direction

and outlook. I see a therapist as well and I must say, I leave Gus's sessions feeling just as motivated and with more personal insight, as I do when I leave therapy."
- Kathryn P.

"Sometimes the first step is the hardest, or we hit a roadblock by ourselves and Altas Readings has helped me to not only reach my goals, but helped me recognize where my faults and traits that hindered my abilities lied and, develop strategies to cope with and overcome my hindered abilities.
- Christina N.

"In the months that I have worked with Gus, I have experienced such a difference in my mindset and overall perspective. Whereas I felt somewhat pushed around by life and wholly out of control of my day-to-day prior to starting life coaching, Gus has helped me to recognize/start the process to self-understanding and to garner the confidence to confront issues head on, not only in the world but also within myself. I cannot express how awesome the shift has been in my life and how much I look forward to our sessions each week.

I cannot wait to continue our work together!"
- Christina P.

This book is my personal invitation to explore how life coaching can be a powerful, transformative force in your own life.

How to Use This Book

There is no need to rush! This book is designed to be accessible and reader friendly. To that end, I am intentionally precise, descriptive, and concise. You may find yourself progressing through the pages quickly. I urge you to re-read and take your time unpacking each lesson.

When you choose to implement learning from this book, I suggest you follow the coaching process. In a session, we explore and decide on a course of action related to the your goal for the coming week or two. Then, it is up to you to commit to these actions and record their experiences. I describe coaching as a grand experiment. In order to have a worthwhile experiment, you have to have as many sources of data as possible before you draw a conclusion. It's important to give yourself one or two weeks of intentional, fully committed, practice in order to create a sufficient amount of data to decide whether or not this action has made an impact in your life. This is the coaching method: commit to an action, trust in the process, and see it through for one or two weeks. Gather your results and experiences, and make your conclusions about how these actions have impacted your life.

Chapter 1
What is Life Coaching?

"Your life does not get better by chance. It gets better by change." – Jim Rohn

Life coaching is described as working with clients in a stimulating and innovative process that motivates them to realize their full potential on both a personal and professional level. Coaching frequently reveals previously undiscovered sources of creativity, productivity, and leadership.

In everyday terms, life coaching is a transformative process that connects you with the best version of yourself and teaches you how to lead from that place. By working with a life coach, you are committing to honest conversation, self-discovery, and actions that push you outside of your comfort zone.

The practice of coaching has two superpowers: opportunity and choice. Everyone has shared their dreams and life ambitions over margaritas with their best friends. These goals are tangible and strong that night, but seem to crumble to sand when the sun comes up. Life coaching reinvigorates these goals, creating a space for them to exist, and exploring why they are important. Life coaches will help you explore what changes if you accomplish these goals. Together, you will envision how you will be different in the future having fully realized your goals. When you have a clear understanding of what values these goals are aligned with and why it is important, the coach can open the discussion up to opportunity. You will explore where there are current opportunities to step closer to these goals.

Life coaching plays an important, indispensable role in my own life. Coaching provides me a space to just be. I have open, honest discussions with my coach around what I truly want, outside of the theater of the every-day. In each session, I enter into a special space, separate from the world, where I can sit at the core of who I am and see the path in front of me. Accountability has been the greatest benefit I've experienced through coaching. Knowing I have someone believing me, holding me accountable to the actions I am committing to, and ready to debrief the lessons I'm learning, gives me the support I need to do things I previously considered impossible.

Life Coaching vs Therapy vs Consulting

Three common practices that are often considered in the same grouping are life coaching, therapy, and consulting. While there are commonalities between each practice, they are ultimately different and distinct. Each practice has its unique approach and benefits. Understanding what each practice offers can help you decide if coaching is right for you. I describe each practice like neighboring countries on the same continent.

Let's try out another metaphor: your goal is to learn how to ice skate.

You go to a consultant and say, "I want to learn how to ice skate." The consultant will get key information from you, including the type of ice skates you own and how you intend to use them – exercise, figure skating, hockey, speed skating. The consultant will write up a manual detailing how to put on the skates, generate speed, move forwards and backwards, etc. As they hand it to you, the consultant explains that if you read and follow this manual step-by-step you will successfully ice skate.

You go to a therapist and say, "I want to learn how to ice skate." The therapist will invite you into their office, offer you a seat, and begin exploring your relationship to ice skating. Have you tried to ice skate in the past? What comes up for you when you revisit that experience? What fears are holding you back in the present? The therapist's goal is to reconcile these past experiences and fears so that you have a solid foundation to stand on in order to begin learning how to ice skate.

You go to a life coach and say, "I want to learn how to ice skate." The life coach will ask if you have a pair of skates. You grab your skates and meet the coach at the local ice skating rink. The coach instructs you to put on the skates and meet them on the ice. They hold your hands and tell you to start pushing off the ice with your skates. The coach explains that they will hold you up and skate next to you while you find your balance. The coach will continue to skate next to you until you feel comfortable doing it by yourself.

All three practices will help you achieve your goal of ice skating. It is up to you to explore and decide which approach is most aligned with your goals.

What Life Coaching Does Not Do

Life coaches are ready to hold your hand as you ice skate, help you keep your balance, and practice skating until you're comfortable enough to do it all by yourself. With respect to therapy, consulting, and other helping disciplines, it is important to acknowledge what is outside the scope of life coaching.

Life coaching is not a replacement for mental health counseling. A life coach is not equipped to manage the mental health of their clients. Unless otherwise stated, life coaches are not trauma counselors, therapists, psychiatrists, or social workers.

Life coaching is not a replacement for medical or legal advice. A life coach, unless otherwise stated, is not a licensed medical doctor or attorney. Many coaches will have a network of practitioners to refer you to if you are asking for services outside of their focus.

Life coaching is not advice. A coach will never tell you what to do. Instead, a coach's goal is to help you explore the possibilities, choose which path best aligns with your goal, and then create actionable steps that move you along that path. If you are looking for someone to give you advice, share their experience, and help lead you down the same path they found success on, I suggest exploring consulting and mentoring opportunities.

When to See a Life Coach

A life coach will co-create an action-oriented process for making your goals a reality. Coaching requires a commitment to action, pushing yourself outside of your comfort zone, and uncovering limiting beliefs. You are called to tap into your bravery and experience how amazing your life can truly be!

Does this make you feel excited? Does this make you feel overwhelmed? Although my intention, and the intention of any coach, is to help you reach your goals, the timeline at which that happens is always up to you. You're the one ice skating. You are skating at the speed that's comfortable for you and moving in your chosen direction. I am simply helping you keep balanced and upright.

In this way, the scope of coaching is unique to each person. The process may be unique to each goal. This adaptability is an application of choice. *Choice*, in coaching, is the recognition that in any given moment, you have the ability and the authority to choose. When it comes to reaching your goals, a coach will help you see where you are at choice. There are no wrong choices, only choices that are aligned or unaligned with your goal.

If you are ready to be at choice, ready to challenge yourself to get out of your comfort zone, and take actionable steps towards your goal, then a life coach will be a great partner on your journey.

How Life Coaching Works

Getting Started Self-Coaching

During the journey of personal and professional transformation, you are going to learn how to effectively self-coach. This is the action of ice skating with a metal skate trainer to help you balance. This learning is experiential, based on your current goals, obstacles, and unique approach to each situation. Part of working with a coach is learning about and strategizing your personal style of problem-solving. Coaching succeeds in supporting this learning because sessions are always client focused. Even though I am confident in Gus-style problem-solving and I know what works best for me, it would be a massive disservice to my clients if I expected all of them to think and act the same way I do. Remember, unlike consulting or mentorship, a coach is not going to tell you what to do.

Self-coaching is a powerful practice that you can get started with today. You are powerful, resourceful, and full of wisdom. The following skills and practices are going to help you connect with that innate wisdom. These are common skills you will learn about and practice during coaching. The information here will help you get started exploring some of these topics on your own.

As I described earlier, coaching is a grand experiment. When you choose to turn this learning into action, I suggest committing to practicing for one or two weeks. Anytime you start practicing a new skill, the first few times will be clumsy. By the fourth or fifth time you practice, you are going to be implementing all you've learned and begin to move forward with more confidence. Trust in yourself and trust in the process. This powerful commitment to yourself will pave the way for powerful transformation.

Chapter 2
The Emotions as Messages

"Emotional intelligence is the ability to sense, understand, and effectively apply the power and acumen of emotions as a source of human energy, information, connection, and influence." — *Robert K. Cooper. Ph.D.*

Your body is capable of processing immense amounts of information. In a study published in the journal *Scientific Reports* in 2016, scientists found that the human brain can take in, "60 bits [of information] per second (bps) for attention, decision-making, perception, motion, and language, and up to 10^6 bps for sensory processing" (Wu, et al. 2016).[1] According to this study, despite the ability to take in these extreme levels of information, our conscious mind can only process about 50-60bps. Our subconscious mind steps in to process the rest. This subconscious information can manifest as instinct, feelings of knowing, and emotions.

Each emotion is unique and can contain within it powerful information to guide you along your path. By treating emotions in this manner, you are acknowledging each feeling, honoring yourself, and creating a safe space to explore your experience.

This practice will create a greater level of trust within yourself and a greater sense of self-confidence. By asking powerful questions of each emotion, you can explore what important information is present and how you can best move forward.

1. Wu T, Dufford AJ, Mackie MA, Egan LJ, Fan J. The Capacity of Cognitive Control Estimated from a Perceptual Decision Making Task. Sci Rep. 2016 Sep 23;6:34025. doi: 10.1038/srep34025. PMID: 27659950; PMCID: PMC5034293.

Anger

Anger is a physical and fiery emotion. Healthy expressions of anger help identify your sense of self. When you know who you are, you consciously and unconsciously set up boundaries or expectations. Anger can be an alarm system, letting you know that a boundary has been crossed, either by someone else or by yourself. When you are experiencing anger, the powerful questions you need to ask of yourself are:

What needs to be mended?

What boundary must be enforced?

Connecting with that anger and asking, "What needs to be mended?" can alert you to where a trespass occurred and how to mend that boundary. Enforcing boundaries can feel uncomfortable at first. Many of us have been taught to be flexible and accessible, even when it makes us uncomfortable. Identifying "What boundary must be enforced?" is a powerful act of self-care. You are standing up for yourself, your values, and your self-worth. I find internal boundaries to be the most difficult to uphold, because many of us want to be non-confrontational and approachable, often at the expense of our own needs. To combat this, I challenge clients to imagine internal boundaries as yellow police tape with DO NOT CROSS printed across in big black letters.

Sadness

Sadness is a watery emotion that wells up and begs to be expressed. Sadness is one of the most common emotional experiences, but it is often overlooked or misunderstood. This emotion can feel like you are totally submerged, where the only recourse is to cry. Sadness can feel like a pit or a hole, like a part of you has been ripped out, or like a subtle nudge towards letting something go and moving on.

Henry Ford said, "Failure is simply the opportunity to begin again, this time more intelligently." Sadness is your body's internal message to start again. It is showing you what is no longer working, how you can let go of it, and how to move forward with strength and authority. The powerful questions to ask sadness are:

What can be let go?

What needs to be renewed?

Sadness is alerting you to a belief, a practice, a relationship, or an expectation that is not serving you. Continuing to hold onto that will only hold you back. When you let go of what you're holding onto, you can find a renewal of spirit. You feel lighter and more like yourself. You feel energized to move on. Asking, "What needs to be renewed?" will help you direct this energy towards new goals.

Sadness can ask a lot of you. Sadness is inherently asking you to step outside your comfort zone, take a risk, and enter into spaces you've never been before. It is very easy to ignore sadness and find coping mechanisms to get you through, because the thought of changing is far scarier than staying where you are. These coping mechanisms can be a subtle quicksand. Before you know it, you're too deep to pull yourself out. Trust in your own bravery and courage. When you honor the message of sadness, you are honoring yourself.

Fear

Fear is, in itself, a scary emotion. Fear turns your legs into lead, the ground into quicksand. Fear sends your heartbeat into a frenzy. You start hyperventilating and sweating. You get nauseous. Fear is by no means an enjoyable experience. Due to these jarring physical expressions, many of us have been taught to avoid fear entirely.

Fear represents change, danger, uncertainty, mystery, and the unknown. It is human nature to want to stay in your comfort zone. Within this warm, safe space you know what to expect. You may even have a certain amount of control over what happens. When you can correctly predict what happens there's no need to worry about the unexpected. But when you stand in your comfort zone, steadfast against the tides of change, you deny yourself the chance to grow and learn.

Fear is your body's natural expression of instinct and intuition. Fear is alerting you to change. This can be a change in your physical environment, a change in your body, changes at work or school, or a change in your life path. To help you see these changes objectively and move forward with confidence, fear is giving you a universal stop sign. Now you have the opportunity to slow down, objectively look around you, and make sure you have all the resources you need to be successful before moving forward. The powerful questions to ask fear are:

What is my intention?

What actions do I need to take?

Fear will bring you back to your drive, your WHY. What pushes you along this path? Does that intention still resonate with you? Is the change in front of you aligned with that intention? What actions do you need to take to further that intention? This emotion requires courage: the courage to not ignore the fear or act in spite of it, but to listen to it. With courage you

How Life Coaching Works

can truly face your fear, ask it "What is my intention?" and "What actions do I need to take?" so that you can be confident in moving forward.

Envy

Envy is an emotional expression that conveys your relationship with the people around you.

Comparative thought is the narrow blade that envy thrives on. This can be a slippery slope beginning with comparing yourself to someone else and ending with putting yourself down because you are not an exact copy of that person. Envy is an emotion that typically carries a negative connotation. Comparison is often seen as the enemy of progress. When envy is honored in a healthy way, there are powerful messages found there.

Envy is alerting you to an imbalance. This imbalance relates to how you see yourself compared to the world around you. Without context and objectivity, the comparison brought on by envy can be debilitating. Clients search for meaning in why they feel so upset when they are envious of their coworker or neighbor. Instead of endlessly circling "why", explore envy from the perspective of a toddler in the insatiable "mine" stage. This toddler will claim everything as "mine" and if you have something they can't have, a catastrophic meltdown will occur. Envy will often present itself from the space of our inner child. It's best to react to it in a similar fashion. The powerful questions to ask envy are:

What about this comparison is exciting to me?

How will my experience be different if I have "it"?

The information available through envy can provide a new perspective into what is important to you right now. By investigating these feelings, you will discern what is coming from that inner child's "mine" voice, and what is a beneficial comparison that leads to learning. Focusing on "How will my experience be different if I have 'it'?" will reveal the substance, or lack thereof, in this comparison and how you can take steps to fulfill this need within your life.

Chapter 3
Skills for Growth

Don't be afraid. Be focused. Be determined. Be hopeful. Be empowered. — Michelle Obama

The power of coaching is based on intentional, aligned, action towards your goal. In a perfect world, the path to your goals would be free of distractions and setbacks. In reality, there are distractions left and right that will try to pull your focus. The skills discussed in this chapter are your defense against these distractions. The practices of affirmations, setting healthy boundaries, and holding others fully responsible, will help you keep your balance and stay at choice. You will be creating a strong foundation within yourself, armed with affirmations to keep your goal in sight, boundaries to keep your balance on your journey, and healthy attachments by holding others fully responsible making you unstoppable. Take time to explore how the following practices work in your life, what results you experience, and how you could tailor these skills for your best results.

Affirmations

Affirmations are positive statements of empowerment and encouragement. These statements can assist you in overcoming self-defeating and pessimistic thoughts. Affirmations are a mental exercise to strengthen your mindset and fortify your outlook. When practiced by writing down or speaking aloud often, you are actively reinforcing this new state of being within your mind.

Affirmations are powerful in their simplicity, versatility, and individuality. You can create an affirmation for nearly anything. The empowering statement doesn't have to make sense to the masses, as long as it is impactful for you. Practicing repeating affirmations can be done in the quiet moments throughout your day, without the need for tools or meditation. Reciting affirmations or writing them down can be an inconspicuous activity, allowing you to practice without anyone else knowing what you're doing. Practice at work, at the gym, in line at the grocery store. This practice creates a foundation of self-love and trust that can lead to great change in your life. Affirmations help you believe in your own potential and the potential for opportunities to manifest in your life.

Do they really work? Yes. Affirmations alone may not be the cure-all for most people, but incorporating these powerful statements into your routine, alongside your other personal growth initiatives, will likely return positive results. Ralph Waldo Emerson wrote, "You are what you think." Your thoughts shape your reality.

Let's explore the difference between these two affirmations:

I am successful.

May I be successful.

In my coaching practice, I lead clients in crafting affirmations that start with "may I" as opposed to the classic "I am". The traditional "I am" affirmation creates a rigid expectation for your daily experience. In the above example, "I am successful" offers only one acceptable outcome. This sharp line can cause feelings of failure or inadequacy when you don't fully live up to that expectation.

"May I" is a modern form of affirmation. Creating an affirmation beginning with "may I" builds in kindness, understanding, and opportunity into your practice. When you focus on creating opportunities, there is no failure. If you don't succeed to the level you expect, there is no reason to get down on yourself. Learn what you can from that experience and trust that another opportunity to express that affirmation is just around the corner. Let this type of affirmation be a gentle invitation to step outside your comfort zone towards your goal.

When creating affirmations, focus on language that is present tense, positive, and unique to you. Encapsulate your desire or the vision you want to see made manifest in a concise sentence. Explore the difference between "I am" and "may I" affirmations within your own life. You may find that the traditional expectations around "I am" offer the perfect structure for you to achieve your goals. Conversely, the gentle invitation of "may I" can be the accessible, non-threatening encouragement needed to take the next step on your journey.

Setting Healthy Boundaries

A strong, healthy boundary is an important act of self-care. Boundaries are the limits and guidelines you create to safely interact with the world. These rules are the imaginary lines that define your individuality, authority, and responsibility. Through boundaries you establish who you are in different situations.

Healthy boundaries are crucial to a strong, grounded, and supported journey towards your goals. In order to be connected to your best self and lead from that space, you need to be clear on your individuality, authority, and responsibility. A healthy boundary has four components: clearly defined, easily communicated, a simple response, and a set consequence.

For a boundary to be clearly defined, it should be able to be expressed in a concise present tense sentence. For example, "I don't usually answer my phone after 10:00pm," is not as strong as "I do not answer my phone after 10:00pm." In one sentence, the *who*, *what*, and *when*, are clearly defined. Both for your benefit and the people who will be subjected to this boundary, the language should be as direct as possible.

A concise and direct boundary is easily communicated. This is a powerful opportunity to craft a boundary that is understandable without room for misinterpretation. For example, "I don't usually answer my phone after 10:00pm," might leave someone thinking that they are the exception to this rule. The boundary, "I do not answer the phone after 10:00pm" is ironclad, with no room for misunderstanding.

A clearly defined and easily communicated boundary deserves a simple response. For example, in response to "I do not answer my phone after 10:00pm," you are asked why? "I prioritize my sleep," constitutes a simple response. Creating these responses is part of creating a healthy boundary because it stops the common urge to overexplain in order for the other party to understand. A healthy boundary does not need to be understood, only respected.

Now you are ready to set a consequence for your boundary. Any parent will be familiar with this step. You tell your child, "These are your chores this week. If you don't do them, you lose your video game privileges." There is a clear understanding of what needs to be done and what happens if it's not completed. Consequences for your boundaries will vary widely for each situation. It is important to identify these actions during the creation of the boundary so you have a plan in place. Let's create a consequence for the example, "I do not answer my phone after 10:00pm." When a person repeatedly breaks this boundary, the consequence you have in place may be to block their number. If this person is unable to respect your personal time boundaries, then they no longer have access to you in that way. I challenge you to stand tall and lead from your space of authority. The consequence does not have to be shared when you explain your boundary, but should be enforced. Upholding your boundaries, and enacting the consequences therein, is a powerful act of self-care.

Holding Others Fully Responsible

Holding others fully responsible is a secret weapon in coaching. This is one of the most impactful lessons I learned through CTI Co-Active Coaching. On the surface, this practice sounds simple. You live and work in spaces with adults who are able to be responsible for themselves. Yet, many of us feel compelled to take on the responsibility of others.

Think back to a time when you stepped in and worked on a coworker's project or told a friend what they should say to their cheating ex. These experiences can be accompanied with thoughts like, "If I don't do it then it won't get done" or "When this happened to me, I should have...." When you make these choices, you are taking responsibility away from others and assuming a role that does not belong to you. You are not giving the other party the time and space to tap into their own innate knowledge and decide which path forward will be best for them. These actions often leave you feeling drained, taken advantage of, and frustrated.

Supporting others as fully responsible creates a healthy style of attachment. You are embracing the individuality of each person, including their skills and unique ways of problem-solving. It allows you to be bold, creative, and resourceful in your relationships. You are inviting others to fully embrace themselves and stand in their full authority.

Maintaining this practice requires holding yourself fully responsible. You are tapping into your own skills and unique methods of problem-solving. Understanding how this boundary shifts depending on your situation is important. When you feel the urge to take a role in someone else's responsibility, ask the other person, "What do you need right now?" Let them discover and advocate for themselves. Offer yourself that same space and authority by asking yourself, "What do I need right now?" when you feel the need to relinquish your responsibility to someone else. Clearly defining your responsibilities will mitigate burnout and overwhelm and the negative feelings of overextending yourself.

Chapter 4
The 5 Keys of Listening

"Listening is a magnetic and strange thing, a creative force. The friends who listen to us are the ones we move toward. When we are listened to, it creates us, makes us unfold and expand." – Karl A. Menniger

Listening is a powerful skill that unlocks deep and honest communication. Truly listening is an act of selflessness, where you put aside your current experiences, and devote yourself to the conversation at hand. Your ability to listen can be inhibited by thoughts, insecurities, and biases. The more you understand yourself, the more you are able to create an open and empathetic space to listen and support others.

The entirety of life coaching is built on the skills of listening. The life coach needs to be present and connected to the client in order to fully support their growth. On the client's side, powerful listening not only connects the client to the coach and the conversation at hand, but also with themselves and the internal messages coming up during the session. When both life coach and client are connected and listening to each other, the space for vulnerability, honesty, and growth is created.

These five keys of listening will help you engage in deeper conversation that ensures both yourself and the speaker are heard, understood, and validated.

Key No. 1
Be Fully Present!

Think back to a time when you've intended to have an important conversation, but the other party is engaged with their email, messages on their phone, or the television. How productive was that conversation? How validated did you feel? The act of being present in conversation is a simple but effective way to begin achieving deeper levels of listening.

Being fully present means more than reducing distractions and focusing on the conversation at hand. If you are in-person, sit in a space that is quiet and peaceful. Put your phone away. Work on making meaningful eye contact. Let your body language reflect your presence in listening. Mirror the speakers' position, hand gestures, expressions.

If you're on the phone, stick to one task. Phone calls, especially talking hands free, offer a lot of opportunity for distraction through keeping your hands busy with dishes, laundry, or checking email. This activity can cause extra noise and chip away at the sense of connection between parties. Challenge yourself to be present and focused.

Key No. 2
Listen to Understand!

A large portion of the conversations you have throughout the day focus on listening to respond. When you go to the coffee shop in the morning, the focus of the conversation is to listen to respond with your coffee order. Many of the conversations around the office are structured in the same way. What time is the meeting? What do you need me to bring to the conference? When do you need these reports? The goal is to give the other party the specific information needed and move on.

When you practice listening to understand, you are making a conscious effort to slow down and comprehend what is being shared. This action creates a safe space within the conversation. Listening to understand means there is no agenda between parties. No one person is trying to convince the other of a certain perspective. No one is wrong and feeling defensive about criticism. As a safe space, both parties can be vulnerable, allowing themselves to be open and honestly share their experiences. It is in these deep connections that learning and growth thrive.

Key No. 3
Be Curious!

A surefire way to end a conversation is to ask yes/no questions. For example, "Do you like Mondays?" The two paths available to answer that question, yes or no, are finite paths. This is like hitting a dead-end while driving. There is no path forward. Finite questions can show a lack of interest and will lead the conversation to a close.

An open-ended question invites the other party to share more of their personal experience. Lean into your natural curiosity and it will always lead the conversation deeper. Each open-ended question is like a fork in the road, every direction representing a path available in this conversation. Staying curious is a great way to create space for other people to fully express themselves and their ideas. This practice also connects with the first key, being fully present. Intentionally asking open-ended questions helps you shift focus onto the other party and stay present.

Key No. 4
Patience!

Patience is the recognition that everyone operates in their own unique way. Some people process and understand situations quickly. Other people need time to process in order to find the right words and examples to get their point across. Practicing patience in conversation is often found in silence. Let there be silence. This ensures that those who need it can gather their thoughts together without feeling rushed.

Patience can also be present by allowing others to advocate for the space and time they need to process appropriately. One of the most powerful ways you advocate for yourself is by saying, "I need to think about this. Can I get back to you at the end of the day?" Here, you are honoring your own patience. You are allowing yourself the space to fully understand what is being asked and shared with you before responding. If you are on the other side of this conversation, you are honoring patience by allowing this other party the processing time they need.

Creating space for others to express themselves includes silence, space, and time. Slow down and be open to conversing with others at their speed.

Key No. 5
Summarize!

Summary already happens in casual conversation. You repeat back details you've heard or make a call back to a joke shared earlier in the conversation. This skill becomes a key to listening when you choose to use summary intentionally.

When summary is used to further the deep connection you've created in conversation, you may say, "I'm hearing a lot of theme x and theme y. This is how I see these themes relating to the topic." This interjection offers understanding, furthers connection, and creates an opportunity for correction. One of the superpowers of summary is making sure the other party is clearly expressing themselves. Now you've opened up a space to pause, assess what has been shared, check for understanding, and then move forward with confidence.

How Life Coaching Works

Becoming a better listener is a powerful skill that will help you as a partner, a friend, a coworker, a manager, and beyond. You will find yourself being more focused in conversations, building stronger relationships, and processing information faster and with more accuracy. As with all of the skills described in this book, learning to be a better listener is a continuous process. New experiences will lead you to learn new lessons and new ways to apply these skills. Be open, stay curious, and trust in yourself.

Chapter 5
Coaching Questionnaire

"What you do makes a difference, and you have to decide what kind of difference you want to make." –Jane Goodall

Now, you may be ready to work with a professional coach. This questionnaire is designed to help you get focused on what you want to bring to your first coaching session. Answer each question honestly, but know that coaching is transformation. These answers represent a stop on your journey, not the destination. As you continue along this journey, it may be insightful to return to this questionnaire after three or six months of coaching and explore how your answers have changed and acknowledge what growth you've experienced.

A copy of this questionnaire is available at www.atlasreadings.com/book. Download and print out as needed.

On a scale from 1 – 10 (10 being the highest), rate the following:

1. I am satisfied with my career.

   ① ② ③ ④ ⑤ ⑥ ⑦ ⑧ ⑨ ⑩

   What is working well right now?

   What do you want to change or improve?

2. I am satisfied with the amount of fun in my life.

①②③④⑤⑥⑦⑧⑨⑩

What do you do for fun right now?

What's possible with more fun in your life?

3. I am satisfied with my romantic relationships.

①②③④⑤⑥⑦⑧⑨⑩

What is working well right now?

What do you want to change or improve?

4. I am satisfied with my personal growth.

   ① ② ③ ④ ⑤ ⑥ ⑦ ⑧ ⑨ ⑩

   What's some recent growth, project, or realization you're proud of?

   What's possible with greater levels of personal growth?

5. I am satisfied with my relationships with my family and friends.

   ① ② ③ ④ ⑤ ⑥ ⑦ ⑧ ⑨ ⑩

   What is working well right now?

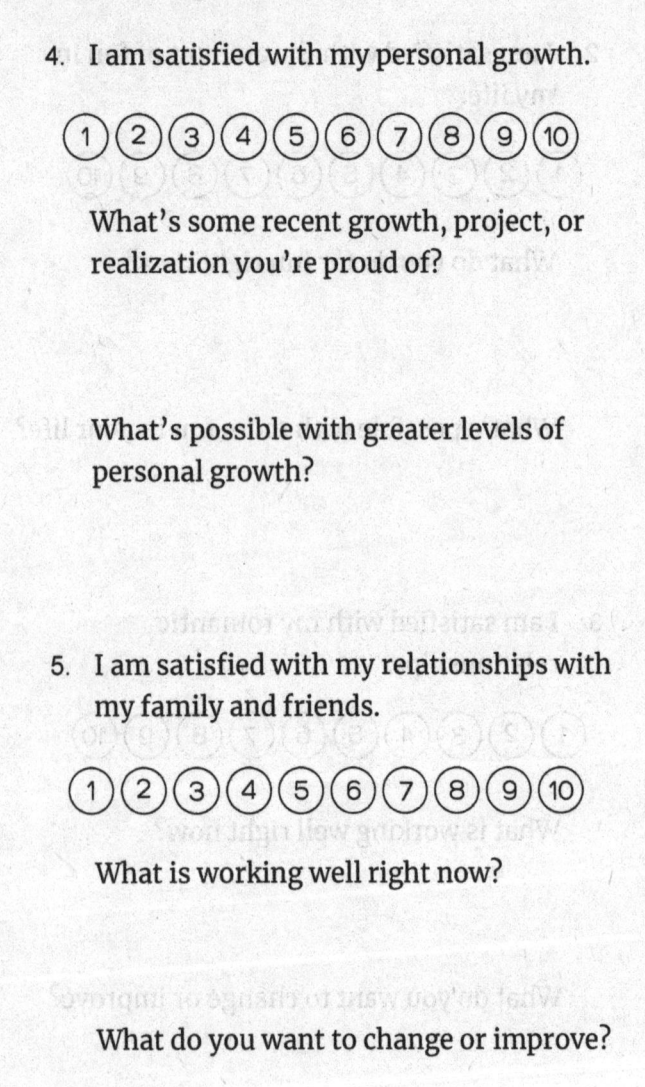

   What do you want to change or improve?

6. I am satisfied with my work/life balance.

① ② ③ ④ ⑤ ⑥ ⑦ ⑧ ⑨ ⑩

What is working well right now?

What is possible with a more equitable work/life balance?

7. I am satisfied with my creative expression.

① ② ③ ④ ⑤ ⑥ ⑦ ⑧ ⑨ ⑩

How do you express creativity right now?

What's possible when you express more creativity in your life?

8. I am satisfied with my relationship with myself.

   ① ② ③ ④ ⑤ ⑥ ⑦ ⑧ ⑨ ⑩

   What is working well right now?

   What is possible with a greater relationship with yourself?

9. I am satisfied with my physical environment.

   ① ② ③ ④ ⑤ ⑥ ⑦ ⑧ ⑨ ⑩

   What is working well right now?

   What do you want to change or improve?

Optional:

10. I am satisfied with
    _____ (fill in
    the blank)

①②③④⑤⑥⑦⑧⑨⑩

What is working well right now?

What do you want to change or improve?

About the Author

I grew up in a house with a messy kitchen, full of leftover science experiments. The dining room table was splattered with watercolors and clay. Yarn and knitting needles were strewn across the couches. This was a house that celebrated passion and inspiration, and welcomed creative solutions.

As a professional, I carry that attitude in my heart. I understand the importance of learning how things are traditionally done, but I never let that box me in. Following my inspiration and trusting my heart, as I was taught to growing up, has given me the tools I need to navigate through transitions, challenges, and celebrations.

As an empath, I believe strongly in boundaries. These commitments help define how we interact with the world and how the world interacts with us. I believe a strong set of boundaries helps you in your professional life, as well as your personal life, and sets the stage for clear communication.

I currently live in New Jersey with my 2-year old Saint Bernard, named Oliver. These last few years have not been easy, but I continue to fall back on my strongest quality: resilience. Resilience doesn't mean it's always easy, or I always look on the bright side. It's quite the opposite. But when you are faced with the difficult or you can't help but feel hopeless, resilience means you trust in what's to come.

It all works out in the end. And if it hasn't worked out, then it's not the end.

Professional Background

- ACC, Associate Certified Coach, via the International Coaching Federation, September 2022
- CPCC, Co-Active Professional Certified Coach, via CTI Co-Active Coaching, August 2022
- Dual Bachelors of Arts in Biological Anthropology
- Published writer in local and international print and digital
- Podcast writer and host

How Life Coaching Works

CPSIA information can be obtained
at www.ICGtesting.com
Printed in the USA
LVHW091549261122
733857LV00016B/1608

9 781087 986135